MAXIM'S PUT-DOWNS, PRANKS & PICK-UP LINES
BECAUSE EVERY JOKE NEEDS A BUTT—BUT IT SHOULDN'T BE YOU

BY THE EDITORS OF MAXIM

DDM Press

DDM Press
1040 Avenue of the Americas
New York, NY 10018
212-302-2626
ISBN 0-9675723-4-7
For more information about Maxim Books, call 877-212-1937.

MAXIM's Put-downs, Pranks and Pick-up Lines
©2000 DDM Press
Photographs ©2000 DDM Press

All rights reserved. No part of this publication may be reproduced or transmitted in any form or by any means, electronic or mechanical, including photocopy, recording or any other information storage and retrieval system without the written permission of the publisher.

Portions of this text have been adapted from *Maxim* and *Stuff* magazines.

Maxim and *Stuff* are registered trademarks of Dennis Publishing, Inc.

Printed in the United States of America.

MAXIM's Put-downs, Pranks and Pick-up Lines

Senior Writer	Amy Spencer
Designer	Jonathan Stern
Photo Editor	Loretta Black
Associate Editor	Sky Shineman
Copy Editors	Tom Brown, Steve Gordon

DDM Press

Chairman	Felix Dennis
President	Stephen Colvin
Chief Financial Officer	Paul Fish
Publisher	Steven Kotok
Group Creative Director	Keith Blanchard
Editor	Leslie Yazel
Production Manager	Lou Terracciano
Direct Marketing Manager	Joanna Molfetta
Directors	Robert G. Bartner, Peter Godfrey

There's nothing standing in between you and being the partymaster.

It's admirable to be respected at the office, but when it comes down to it, every guy would rather be czar of the bar than king of the copier. You know, that guy who shows up at a party and commands attention from every person in the joint. The guy who tells all the right stories, makes all the winning bets, has all the right comebacks—and turns even the ice princess perched at the end of the bar into a gooey mess of giggles. He'd be a real bastard if he weren't so damn funny. Of course, the only way to make sure you're not the butt of his next joke is to make sure that guy is you. So are you ready for insults to fit every occasion? An endless backlog of bar tricks that will make even smart babes "ooh" and "ah" with wonder all the way to your bed? Here's a simple guide to taking down the next jerkoff who says "What are you looking at?" without stammering or stuttering ever again. Ready to be the guy who steps up to charm the capri pants off the gorgeous model your barfly buddies were too chicken to even approach? Read on and get the guaranteed home court advantage wherever beer is served.

INSULTS

Being Mr. Nice Guy is an admirable way to win friends and influence people. But we all know that the real way to another's heart is cold, back-stabbing laughter at the expense of other people. The next time you're in a bar with your buddies insulting every fat, ugly moron you know, send them to their knees with clever commentary like this. (And if you're a fat and ugly moron, just be sure to speak up first.)

SNUBS FOR ALL OCCASIONS

You can insult people the bologna-and-white-bread way—or you can do it in Dagwood style.

INSTEAD OF SAYING "YOU TALK TOO MUCH," SAY...

"You could talk your head off and you wouldn't even notice."

"Hearing you talk is like reading a history book—you're always repeating yourself."

"You want some cheese to go with that whine?"

"You know how some things go without saying? You never do."

"Your head comes to a nice point. How come you never do?"

"I don't mind if you keep talking, if you don't mind that I'm ignoring you."

"Free speech is a right, not an obligation."

INSTEAD OF SAYING "YOU'RE UGLY," SAY...

"Is that your face or did your neck throw up?"

"I feel like I owe you the price of admission to be able to look at your face."

"You weren't the only one crying like a baby the day you were born. Your parents were, too."

"Want to see something funny? Look in the mirror."

"You're so ugly your parents rubbed roast beef on your face so the dog would play with you."

"I was sorry to hear about the accident you had as a child. Being born, I mean."

"Is that your nose or are you eating a gourd?"

"How can you be a nature lover when it did that to your face?"

"The last time I saw a face like yours, the zookeeper was feeding it mice."

"Have you ever thought about being in the movies? Your face would look much better in a dark theater."

"Things could be worse: You could be twins."

"You're a perfect argument against cousins marrying each other."

"You're so white it looks like you donated blood and forgot to say 'when'."

"When you were born, the doctor slapped your mom."

INSTEAD OF SAYING "GET THE HELL OUT OF HERE!" SAY...

"I'd like to give you a going-away present...if you promise to go away."

"Don't think it hasn't been really great knowing you—because it hasn't."

"I'd kick you out of here, but I don't believe in cruelty to animals."

"Even people who don't know you don't like you."

"Next time you pass my house—keep going."

"You're the kind of guy that's gonna go places. Don't let us keep you!"

INSTEAD OF SAYING "YOU'RE AN ASSHOLE," SAY...

"Is your family doing well? Or are you still living with them?"

"You're one in a million. Thank God."

"You should leave your ego to science. Maybe they can find a cure for it."

"You're not an asshole like a lot of guys. You're a whole new breed of asshole."

"I don't know what makes you such an asshole, but it obviously works!"

"You'd be a great guy if it weren't for your personality."

"I hope to run into you again sometime—with the front of my car."

INSTEAD OF SAYING "YOU'RE AN IDIOT," SAY...

"You're much better looking when I'm drunk."

"At least you're in good company. Better company than I am."

"You're smarter than you look. I guess you'd have to be."

"It's been nice talking with you. My brain needed the rest."

"You're about as sharp as a bowling ball."

"I guess your brains ran down your dad's leg."

"How long can humans live without a brain? Well, how old are you?"

INSTEAD OF SAYING "YOU'RE FAT," SAY...

"Shut your mouth before someone stuffs an apple in it."

"You've got more chins than a Chinese phone book."

"They say that travel broadens a person. Looks like you've been all over the world."

"You're so fat you've got smaller fat people in orbit around you."

"What's that scent you're wearing...gravy?"

WHEN YOU WANT TO PUT DOWN HER NEW BOYFRIEND, SAY...

"He calls himself an outdoor guy because no one would let him in."

"I heard he's related to royalty: King Kong."

"He's so desperate to be wanted, he robs houses."

"He's so conceited he gets his X-rays retouched."

WHEN SOMEONE IS SINGING AND YOU WANT THEM TO SHUT THE HELL UP, SAY...

"Who sings that song, anyway? Oh yeah—let's keep it that way."

"Do singers run in your family? They should!"

"Do you sing in the shower? I guess you only sing about once a month, then."

DISH IT OUT LIKE A PRO
Learn from these headliners...who did damage with these one-liners.

"You're like a pay toilet, aren't you? You don't give a shit for nothing."
—Howard Hughes on Robert Mitchum

W.C. Fields, on movie mogul Louis B. Mayer's suggestion they play a round of golf:
"My boy, when I want to play with a prick, I'll play with my own."

Sylvester Stallone on his marriage to Brigitte Nielsen:
"I was married by a judge. I should have asked for a jury."

"We live in a country where John Lennon gets six bullets in the chest. Yoko Ono's standing right next to him, not a fucking bullet. Will you explain that to me, God?" —Denis Leary

CBS sportscaster Frank Glieber, on coworker Billy Packer's new sports jacket: "Who shot the couch?"

"Arnold Schwarzenegger looks like a condom full of walnuts."
—British comedian Clive James

"Every minute this broad spends outside of bed is a waste of time."
—Michael Todd on ex-wife Elizabeth Taylor

"He reminds me of nothing so much as a homeless dog crazed into near dementia by the need to be petted."
—Shakespearean actor Michael Atkinson on Robin Williams

F. Scott Fitzgerald to humorist Robert Benchley:
"Bob, don't you know that drinking is a slow death?"
Benchley: "So? Who's in a hurry?"

"Michael Jackson's album was only called *Bad* because there wasn't enough room on the sleeve for *Pathetic*." —Prince

"Sometimes Howard makes me wish I was a dog and he was a fireplug."
 —Muhammad Ali on Howard Cosell

"It was reported that Barry Manilow was taking a year off to write a Broadway musical...taking a year off from what?"
—Conan O'Brien

"Since light travels faster than sound, some people appear to be bright until you hear them speak."
—Chicago Bull Brian Williams on basketball analyst Isiah Thomas

Jay Leno, on the news of Kathie Lee Gifford's husband, Frank, having an affair: "When Kathy Lee first heard about this she was speechless. So at least something good has come out of it."

"I love his work, but I couldn't be warm to him even if I was cremated next to him."
—Keith Richards on Chuck Berry

"You've got the brain of a four-year-old boy, and I bet he was glad to get rid of it."
—Groucho Marx

"How is it possible to play the harmonica professionally for 30 years and still show no sign of improvement?"
—Music critic David Sinclair on Bob Dylan

Legendary jazzman George Melly, after Mick Jagger explained that the wrinkles on his face were just laugh lines:
"Surely nothing could be *that* funny?"

"Sleeping with George Michael would be like having sex with a groundhog." —Boy George

"I'm not putting Elvis down, but he was a shit-ass, a yellow-belly, and I hated him, the fucker." —Jerry Lee Lewis

"When someone in Green Bay says he has a good wardrobe, it means he has 10 bowling shirts."
—Former Green Bay Packer Greg Koch

"The Kennedys are like the dinosaurs in *The Lost World:* They have big teeth, breed like crazy, and wherever they go women are running and screaming."
—Jay Leno

COMEBACKS

Average time between the second you're insulted and the moment when *you* come up with the perfect comeback: 2 days, 9 hours, and 27 seconds. And what good is it then, when you're surrounded by a band of tan trench coats on the 7 A.M. commuter train? To assure that you'll never be at a loss for words again, here are the comebacks you wish you knew six months ago, and the ones your enemies will wish you never learned…

BE THE COMEBACK KID
Arm yourself with answers to the lamest insults and the stupidest questions.

YOU'RE FAT!
"That's because every time I fuck your mother she makes me sandwiches."

YOU'RE AN IDIOT
"No, I'm just talking like one because it's the only language you understand!"

WHO DO YOU THINK YOU'RE TALKING TO?
"How many guesses do I get?"

WHO ARE YOU CALLING STUPID?
"I don't know, what's your *real* name?"

YOUR CAR'S A PIECE OF SHIT!
"Well, it rides better than your mom!"

HAVEN'T I SEEN YOU SOMEWHERE BEFORE?
"Maybe. Sometimes I get careless where I go."

WHAT WOULD YOU DO WITHOUT ME?
"I could fantasize about that all day."

I'M NOT MYSELF TODAY
"No kidding—we all noticed the improvement."

I HAVE A GREAT IDEA!
"Beginner's luck."

I SHOULD GIVE YOU A PIECE OF MY MIND
"Can you really spare it?"

IGNORANCE IS BLISS
"Yeah, well you must be the happiest person on Earth!"

SORRY, MY MIND WAS WANDERING
"Don't you think it's too small to be out there on its own?"

YOUR MAMA'S SO FAT...
"What do you say we get off moms, 'cause I just got off yours."

FIGHT BACK AND WIN!

With relationship judo, you can roll with her punches and use her own antagonism against her. Here's how.

First, realize that no comeback is more important than one you can use on an accusatory girlfriend. Neutralize her next attack with this three-step technique:

1) agree with her, then...

2) counter her assertion with your own, then...

3) spread your hands helplessly, manage a brave smile, and tell her that men are defenseless without the yielding, nurturing love of women. This trick should get you to first base; you're on your own from there.

She says: "You're sex-obsessed!"

You say:

1) It really must seem that way.

2) But the fact is, it's difficult to get our sexual needs met. It's much easier for women to get laid.

3) All we really want is what everyone wants...to be loved. Hold me.

She says: "Monogamy is not in a man's vocabulary!"

You say:

1) You're right.

2) But isn't monogamy an ideal, a fantasy? Women prefer this fantasy. Men prefer another.

3) Can't you see how lost and frightened we are? Hold me.

She says: "Why are men so phobic about commitment?"

You say:

1) It's hard when you care about somebody and they don't give you what you want.

2) Just as women hate being treated as sex objects, men resent becoming commitment objects.

3) I'm not a doll on a wedding cake. I have feelings and fears. When you press me about commitment, you diminish me in ways I can't even begin to explain. Hold me.

She says: "Men become 'distinguished,' but women get old."

You say:

1) God, I'm as sick as you are of our culture's obsession with youth.

2) But women live an average of seven to 10 years longer than men. That's nearly a 10th of a lifetime!

3) I don't want to die! Hold me.

BAR TRICKS

It's a scientific fact that three out of five nights involving a group of men and alcohol will escalate into some form of making and taking bets. And if you haven't figured it out by now, making a bet is generally more profitable than taking one (unless you enjoy drinking beer backwash full of cigarette ashes). Store these tricks up your sleeve for a night when the beers (and the jokes) are on everyone but you.

PLACE YOUR BAR BETS

You shoot the same old shit with your friends so much, even the barman thinks the stink's getting stale. Work the crowd—or a woman—with these bar challenges.

THE PALM PILOT PUSHOVER

The next time some bulky guy spouts off about how strong he is, place your palm on the top of your head. Then bet him some embarrassing feat (ideally involving him on all fours and a barking sound) that he cannot lift your palm from your head by pushing up on your forearm. Woof woof.

THE CHAMPAGNE DREAMER

Bet some joker you can drink out of a champagne bottle without opening it; he calls bullshit. Have the waiter bring a bottle; then flip it upside down, pour a slug of beer into the hollow on the bottle's bottom and drink up. You've just drunk out of a champagne bottle without opening it.

THE QUARTER QUICKIE

Hand your business card to a woman and say, "I'll bet you a dime that you can't tear this card into four pieces within four seconds. If you can, I'll give you a quarter." After she's rapidly torn the card up, return one of the four pieces to her. And while she's rolling her eyes that you've given her a "quarter" of the card (you know, the piece that has your phone number on it), pocket the dime.

THE QUARTER QUICKIE, PART 2

Place a quarter on the table and cover it with a napkin. Bet the next round of drinks that you can remove the quarter without touching the napkin in any way. While the group discusses how thirsty they are, sneak another quarter in your hand and hold it under the table. Mutter and make incantations over the hidden quarter, then pull your hand from under the table saying, in a fanciful Doug Henning impression, "Either my magic incantation worked, or it's all an illusion!" They won't believe you, of course, and will remove the napkin to check, revealing the first quarter. When they do, grab the coin and win the bet—you never touched a thing.

THE FOOTSIE FOOL

Wager a pint that your friend can't stand against a wall with both his shoulder and the side of his foot touching it, and then lift the other foot for more than .004 seconds. (It seems possible, but try it, it ain't.) It's the easiest beer in the book.

THE ROLLOVER

Place a fiver on the bar. Then take an empty beer bottle and set it upside down on the bill. Make the fantastic assertion that you can remove the currency without touching the bottle or making it fall over. When a sucker bites, grab the bill and slowly roll it. As the rolled edge touches the bottle, it will gradually push the bottle off.

THE VIAGRA SMOKER

If you're a smoker, this is a great way to get back at a guy who's always bumming your butts—and win a beer. Bet him that you can make your cigarette ash hang on longer than his. The trick? Before you bet, straighten out a paper clip and place it lengthwise inside one of your cigarettes. While your friend tries to precariously balance his ash, yours will burn eternal with the support of the clip.

THE SUGAR SMACKER

The next time you're in a restaurant with a couple of smokers and a bowl of sugar cubes (then again, when are you not?), pick up a sugar cube and state that although it's highly flammable, you bet you could hold a flame beneath the cube without burning it. The trick? Move the cube around in an ashtray until it's covered with cigarette ashes, making it inflammable. After you win your bet, drop it in your friend's cup o' joe.

THE FRENCHIE AFFRONT

Everyone hates a boaster. Especially one who claims to do sissy things—like speak French—better than anyone else. Next time interrupt him by saying, "I bet my French accent is 10 times better than yours. Why not let this beautiful young lady be the judge? Well? How about the bet? I'll take five bucks if I'm wrong." "Quelle horreur!" he'll think, as he takes you on. After he's done hacking up his r's, you win the bet because you *are* wrong.

THE NUMBER CRUNCHER

Tell your friend you're going to call out some numbers. Bet that he can't call out the next higher number correctly, without hesitation. Start out by giving some number like 47 and work up to 99. He'll answer 100. Next, say 999. He'll reply 1,000. Finally, throw out the figure nine thousand ninety-nine. Chances are, he'll say 10,000 rather than 9,100. Call him an idiot.

THE BILLY BALDWIN

Want to guarantee that a woman remembers your name? Tell her that some famous actor with the same first name (and who's younger than you) was named after you. She'll be right not to believe you, but go ahead and bet a drink that you can prove it. Then point out that because you were born first, he was clearly named after you. If she's not too disappointed that she won't be invited to the Baldwin brothers birthday bash, tell her the drink's on you.

THE WET HEAD

When the time comes to pay a rude bartender his due, pull this trick on him: Ask for a glass of water, and cover the top of the glass with a coaster. Invert the glass and place it upside down on the bar. Slide the coaster out from beneath the glass and get the hell outta Dodge. It'll be impossible for him to remove the glass without major spillage—hopefully all over his crotch.

THE MATCH POINT

Rip a cardboard match out of a matchbook. Hold it above the table and let it drop. It will land flat on its side. Bet the witnesses they can't make it fall on its edge before you do. When it's your turn, bend it in half before you let it drop.

PRANKS

When you were a kid, you pulled pranks on adults for your own amusement. Now that you're an adult, you would never infringe upon other adults who ask no more than for a life of privacy and peace and quiet promised them in the Constitution. Ha ha ha ha! Here are plenty of ways to annoy the hell out of your friends, co-workers, and neighbors, just like you did in the good ol' days.

10 PRANK PHONE CALLS
For a good time, call the following—and keep calling...

1. Call an escort service and ask for two hours with the best girl. Make it clear that if there's time left over, you want her to spend it cleaning your bathroom. If they say their girls don't do that, start a philosophical argument: Why would a girl who'd have sex for money would feel that scrubbing a toilet is beneath her?

2. Call a tobacconist and say, "Hi, this is Prince Albert. Any calls for me while I was in the can?"

3. Call an undertaker and ask, "Hypothetically, how long could a body buried in a basement go undetected before neighbors pick up the stink?"

4. Call the Q-tips 800 number and say that one of the cotton swab parts just came off in your ear. As they reply, keep shouting, "What? What?! What did you say?"

5. Call the personal ads department of a newspaper or magazine and leave messages for women who say they're looking for "generous" or "financially stable" men. Explain in a British accent that you are a wealthy investor with a slight heart condition and a private jet, and that you're in search of a traveling companion. Leave the phone number of a local homeless shelter or mental hospital.

6. Call your high school English teacher, now in her 70s, and confess that you've burned with desire for her since you were 15 and want to start a phone sex relationship. If she says no, say, "Well, would you know the number for Mr. Pyle, the woodshop teacher?"

7. Call a crime hot line and tell the cops you saw your neighbor wearing a T-shirt that reads "Property of the New York Mets."

8. Call a poison control center. Say you just ate a whole container of Tic Tacs and you feel "all minty" inside.

9. Call the fencing coach at a major university. Ask what's best for keeping your beagle in the yard.

10. Call an addiction hot line and explain that you're hooked on phonics.

THINGS TO DO WHEN YOU'RE BORED

Whenever ennui has you by the short ones, choose an activity from the following list and annoy the hell out of your neighborhood.

1. Go to a hospital. When a surgeon comes out of a successful transplant procedure, pour a big bucket of icy Gatorade over his head.

2. Ask strangers if they have change for a nickel.

3. Set a slinky "walking" down an up escalator in any large department store.

4. Attend an AA meeting. When you're called on, say, "Well, I personally don't have any trouble holding my booze. But the last time my car broke down it took forever to get a tow truck! I mean, what are we paying dues for if that's the kind of service we get?"

5. Empty a gas can and punch a small hole in the side. Fill the can with water and carry it down a busy lunch-hour sidewalk while smoking the biggest cigar you can find.

6. Wear a cheese head constantly for an entire week. Whenever someone comes up and says, "Go Packers!" look at him like you don't know what he's talking about.

7. Tail a stranger for two hours while discreetly talking into the flower on your lapel.

8. Try to wear a suit of armor through a metal detector.

9. Call National Acme. Ask if the company has any products you could use to kill a roadrunner.

10. Before your next party, squeeze little balls of toothpaste onto a silver dish. Let them dry and tell guests they're homemade after-dinner mints.

11. Rush yourself to the ER and explain to the night nurse that you were resting on your leg for a long time and now it feels like pins and needles.

12. Before sitting down on a subway or bus, put a newspaper on the seat. At least once a minute, stand up and turn a page, then sit down again.

13. During a church bingo evening, shout "Pingo!" or "Dingo!" at an arbitrary point in each game. When the other players get mad, patiently explain that it's really their mistake.

14. When you get up to the Burger King counter, ask for directions to another Burger King so you can buy a Whopper. Smile vacantly when they try to explain that all Burger Kings serve the same food. Then insist on those directions again.

15. Purchase a shopping cart full of groceries, and when the bagger asks, "Paper or plastic?" see how long you can hold up the line making up your mind. Then get flustered and try to carry the whole cartful in your arms.

BEAT THE OFFICE BLUES
When your in-box is weighing down your soul, play a few pranks on your colleagues to lift it right back up.

1. Groan out loud while in a bathroom stall (at least one other person must be in the men's room), then say, "Jeez, that burns!"

2. Hand a paper to some office schmuck, tag him and say "You're it," and then run away.

3. Leave a copy of Penthouse Forum (open to a good letter) in the photocopier.

4. Razor blade the erasers off all of some poor sap's pencils.

5. Stick a wad of chewing gum on the underside of the boss' desk.

6. Turn the brightness level on the receptionist's computer monitor all the way down so he or she will think it's broken.

7. In the middle of a meeting, suddenly exclaim, "Yahtzee!"

8. Get at least 10 of your coworkers to high-five you for no reason.

9. For half an hour, whistle the first seven notes of "It's a Small World" every two minutes.

10. Sharpen all of your coworkers' pencils down to tiny stubs.

11. Put your garbage can on your desk. Label it "IN." Leave it there for at least an hour.

12. While riding the elevator, gasp dramatically each time the door opens.

13. Tape your fists à la Rocky with ordinary Scotch tape.

14. Page yourself over the intercom. (Do not disguise your voice.)

15. Ask a male colleague if your ass "looks fat in these pants." If he says no, tell him, "You're just saying that."

16. While everyone is out, leave a carefully formed trail of Cap'n Crunch leading from your boss' office to a fellow employee's door.

17. Remove all the items taped or posted to the wall of some anal-retentive type, then reattach them so they face the wall.

18. With a felt pen, write "SH" in tall block letters on a piece of paper, then tape it over the first two letters of an EXIT sign so that it reads SHIT.

19. Hide a travel-size alarm clock in your boss' desk and set it to go off during his next meeting.

20. Posing as a maître d', call a colleague and tell him he won a lunch for four at a local restaurant. Let him go.

PICKUPS

It's not enough to get a woman's attention. (Heck, pour a beer on her head and you'll get her attention.) The trick is to introduce yourself in such a way that she can't ignore you, won't forget you and—this part's critical—won't think you're an asshole. From showing up at a bar in a pair of pajamas to revealing an embarrassing childhood story to offering her your Pez dispenser, here are plenty of tricks, tactics and words that work.

LINES SO BAD THEY'RE GOOD

We asked three beautiful New York City bartenders to keep a journal of some of the lines men shot at them over a two-week period. Most were cheap and classless. But these 10 cheesy lines actually earned the guys a smile:

1. "Can I be your slave on your next day off?"

2. "Aren't there any child labor laws in this business? What are you, 14?"

3. "You look like the Statue of Liberty holding that tray way up high. Can I call you Liberty? Hell, can I call you?"

4. "Your boyfriend is the luckiest man in the world. But are you happy? Call me."

5. "I'm Steve. Have you ever dated a Steve?"

6. "If you were a booger, I'd pick you first."

7. Him: "Were you talking to me?"
Her: "No."
Him: "Oh. Would you please start?"

8. "This tastes almost as good as you look."

9. "Hey, we have something in common. I'm rich and you're beautiful." (Recommended for guys named Rich.)

10. "Does your boyfriend tell you how beautiful you are every day? 'Cause if he doesn't, I will!"

20 CONVERSATION STARTERS

Any twerp can say hello to a woman. The challenge is to keep the conversation going from that point on. This trivia can help:

1. A pig's orgasm lasts for 30 minutes.
2. Donkeys kill more people every year than plane crashes do.
3. Babies are born without kneecaps, which don't form until children reach two to six years of age.
4. China has more English speakers than the United States.
5. Dueling is legal in Paraguay as long as both parties are registered blood donors.
6. Elephants are the only mammals that can't jump.
7. You share your birthday with at least nine million other people in the world.
8. Some lions mate more than 50 times a day.
9. Our eyes stay the same size from birth, but our nose and ears never stop growing.
10. Stewardesses is the longest word you can type using only the left side of the keyboard.
11. Humans and dolphins are the only species that have sex for pleasure.
12. Reno, Nevada, is west of Los Angeles, California.
13. An ostrich's eye is bigger than its brain.
14. Forty-thousand Americans are injured by toilets every year.
15. Your stomach must produce a new layer of mucus every two weeks or it'll digest itself.
16. Women blink nearly twice as often as men.
17. The male pig has a corkscrew-shaped penis (not unlike his tail), which he slowly winds into the female.
18. The fingerprints of koala bears are virtually indistinguishable from those of humans—so much so, they could be confused at a crime scene, if koalas ever committed crimes.
19. Most hospitals make money by selling umbilical cords. (They're used in vein-transplant surgery.)
20. Carnivorous animals will not eat an animal that has been killed by lightning.

GET YOURSELF A GIMMICK!

You're a face in the crowd. That ain't enough. Try these . . . we bar-tested 'em!

THE PAJAMA GAME

Concept: You go to a bar dressed in jammies and a bathrobe.

Road Tester: Kevin, 32

Road Tested: Kevin walked into a bar with two friends at 8:40 on a Wednesday night, head to toe in nap wear. At 9:06 Kevin got a nibble of female recognition: A girl on her way out noticed him and cracked up. Kevin waved and smiled innocently. "On my way to a slumber party," he called. "Thought I would drop by for a quick drink first." The attention spread. As the hours passed, Kevin fielded comments and come-ons from 26 women. At midnight, he moved to a quintessential beach dive bar, and Kevin was immediately greeted by four more females eager to comment on his getup. "I am so jealous!" squealed one spunky beach girl. "I wish I were wearing that right now!"

Why it works: You are a one-man walking conversation piece. The ensemble shows a woman you have a sense of humor and serious guts. Buddies are a must: Go this alone and everyone will assume premature senility.

BAR-STOOL POETRY

Concept: On a cocktail napkin, jot down a title for a poem, like "My Summer in Spain" or "Why I Love Beer Pretzels." Slide the napkin to your buddy, whose job is to write a poem to fit your title.

Road Tester: Bob, 37

Road Tested: "The joint was packed on the Thursday night I traded quirky verse with my two friends. Within 30 minutes we hit the jackpot. The three girls at the table to our right asked us what we were doing, eager to join in the jocularity. By midnight, these five strangers were huddled over our table with me and my two buddies, laughing as they attempted to read their bar-stool poems in the bar."

Why it works: It's subtle. You're giving women a great reason to come over and ask what you're doing. Then they can join in. "This game works because it goes against the traditional aggressive male role, which many women find threatening," explains Dr. Samuel Shem, a psychiatry professor at Harvard Medical School and author of the gender-issues book *We Have to Talk* (Basic Books, 1998).

QUIZ SHOW

Concept: Bring a deck of cards from a trivia board game—in this case, *Jeopardy!* Whoever answers a predetermined number of questions correctly is bought a drink.

Road Tester: Jason, 29

Road Tested: "My friend Brian and I sat at the bar to be in better view of all the women. In our first at-bat, we went for the direct approach: Brian fanned out five category cards in his hand, extended them toward a blonde and a brunette who were attempting to get seats at the crowded bar and said, 'Ladies, if you can answer a question from any one of these categories, we'll buy you both drinks.'

"They blew the Geography for $200 category, as well as the other questions on the card, so we riffled through the deck and found them a no-lose category.

"A minute later, two hot NYU students left their booth and came up to the bar. 'What are you guys doing?' We started another round. These girls knew their stuff, and by the time we finished, we were all pretty plastered. Just before they took off for the night, both of them gave us their phone numbers."

Why it works: "A game like this says you're interested in her brain, not just her body parts," says Bryan Redfield, who wrote *Bartender's Guide on How to Pick Up Women.* They also perceive the drink as a prize they've earned instead of the come-on it really is.

MAXIM's Put-Downs, Prank's and Pick-up Lines.

THE SUNDAY CROSSWORD PUZZLE

Concept: When you're trolling solo, work a crossword puzzle at the bar.

Road Tester: Steven, 33

Road Tested: "I used the newspaper puzzle so it would look like I had just casually decided to stretch my mind while reading the paper, not like I was some weenie who bought a puzzle book especially for the occasion. I also filled in about a dozen answers at home, and left a few spaces blank that I already knew how to answer, so I could instantly impress a woman.

"It wasn't long before I noticed the girls sitting an empty stool away at the bar sort of checking out what I was doing, so the next time the bartender came over, I asked him if he knew the answer to a clue that had me perplexed about a 1974 Oscar winner. God bless him, he had no idea. A moment later, the girl sitting farther away actually got up and moved around her friend to sit on the empty stool next to me and asked if she could help.

"We never did get the answer to the Oscar question, but to get her number I said, 'Since we can't seem to figure it out, why don't I just fill it in with your phone number?'"

Why it works: The gimmick attracts smart women who like to show off their brains, like hot college chicks.

RULES OF THE GAME

She'll decide in the first 10 minutes whether she'll be writing home to Mom about you. Just incorporate one of these rules—and then point her toward the mailbox.

1. **ALWAYS REVEAL A SECRET:** Start the story, laugh gently, stop for a second and say, 'I can't believe I'm telling you this.' Then fill in the blank. Make it all up if you want to. The important thing is to make her believe that she is the only one you trusted with this tale. It encourages her, in turn, to see you as the only one she would trust to get in her pants. Tailor your confession to the information she has already given you: "I wouldn't want the boys to know, but I'm a total cat guy. They are so soft and fuzzy. I just love them."

2. **ALWAYS TALK ABOUT CLOTHES:** Compliment hers, which shows that you notice. Mention that you've got to do some shopping yourself, which shows that even if she hates how you dress, she can change you.

3. **ALWAYS TELL CHILDHOOD STORIES:** Nothing is more disarming than a nice tale from the good old days. Tell her about your boyhood indiscretions: "Girls were always trying to bring me into the bathroom with them while they peed. I never really understood what was going on." It neatly expresses what a naughty little boy you were without tarnishing your sheen of innocence. You must make her see the outlines of that sweet little boy in your corrupt old man's face. Exercise caution in story selection, however, because tales about how you pooped in your pants because your dad wouldn't pull the car over are going to get you nowhere.

4. ALWAYS ESTABLISH THAT YOU KNOW OTHER WOMEN: Having a woman with you in a friendly capacity means you're not totally inept. If you can't produce one in the flesh, make sure to refer to a wide circle of female friends and acquaintances. "My friend Amanda says…"

5. ALWAYS ASK HER IF SHE WRITES: All women imagine themselves to be creative souls. She will answer either "Yes" or "I've always wanted to, but…"

6. ALWAYS SPEAK IN HUSHED TONES: If you can't come up with a secret, you can still use the voice of secrecy. Even when you're simply stating the obvious, make sure to lower your voice to a gravelly whisper. "The red stool is farther away than that blue one." Your voice may not send shivers down her spine, but that's not the point. Women are always aware of their standing in the eyes of the crowd. Put on a show of great mirth for the assembled masses, then lean down and whisper something quietly, just to her.

7. ALWAYS CARRY A PEZ DISPENSER: Pull it out casually and offer her a candy goiter. The Pez dispenser is like a magic wand.

MAKE 'EM LAUGH
If you want to make a woman laugh, try a few flatulence-free jokes.

CHICK JOKE #1:

The day after the wedding, a woman turns to her new husband and says, "You're a really lousy lover." He looks at her and asks, "How can you tell after just 30 seconds?"

CHICK JOKE #2:

A guy goes to the grocery store. He buys eggs, milk, orange juice, and a package of bacon. He puts his purchases on the belt and fishes around for his money.

As the clerk is ringing them up, she comments, "Wow. Guess you must be single."

Finding nothing about his choices that would lead to this conclusion, the guy replies, "I am single—but how did you know?"

"Because you're ugly."

CHICK JOKE #3:

Two men die and go to heaven. "How'd it happen?" the first man asks the second. "I froze to death," he replies. "How about you?"

"I had a heart attack. I knew my wife was cheating on me, so one day I came home early and ran up to the bedroom. She was alone, reading. I ran downstairs, but no one was hiding there. I sprinted to the attic, and just as I got there, I had a massive heart attack and died."

The second man shakes his head. "That's so ironic," he says. "If you had only stopped to look in the freezer, we'd both still be alive."

FIVE CLOSING REMARKS

Getting her to open up to you is worthless if you don't know how to close the deal. Here's how to exit while keeping the door wide open.

1. "If a guy's friends are leaving and he stays behind to talk to you, there's suddenly a lot of pressure on. He should always leave with his friends. He can simply say he doesn't want to ditch them, then ask if he can call me. He comes off like a good pal and not just someone on the make."
—Diana, 24, New York, NY

2. "The best thing he can do is try to make a date off of our common interests. If we were talking about golf, 'We should go to a driving range sometime' is a great thing to say. It's not like the pressure of a date, more like you're sports companions. If I want to see you, I'll pick up on your invite."
—Phoebe, 32, Westport, CT

3. "Politeness is always a good thing. What's great is a simple handshake and 'I enjoyed meeting you, I'd love to talk to you again,' with a suggestion of a specific exhibition or a show to see is great. That would make me feel like a guy has it together."
—Aimee, 26, Berkeley, CA

4. "If you're inviting her to do something in the future, even if vaguely, it's best not to make it another bar or, even worse, the same bar you're presently in. You seem like you have nothing going on but drinking."
—Wendy, 28, Darien, CT

5. "I used to give out my number, but there are so many damn freaks out there that if I like a guy I'll ask for his number. The coolest thing is if a guy offers me his number. It shows he's not afraid I'll leave him sitting by the phone—he doesn't need to be the one in total control, and that shows confidence. Sexy."
—Marnie, 24, Detroit, MI